# Minimalist Budget Tips

*Simplify Your Money Management*

# Table of Contents

# Introduction

More than just being budget tips for the minimalist, this book is also about the virtues of minimalism. This minimalism is influenced by frugal spending and, in turn, frugal lifestyles are influenced by minimalistic tendencies.

There is a lot that needs to be deciphered and demystified, especially when it comes to understanding the commonly spoken terms of minimalism, budgets, frugalism, debts, and loans and so on. Minimalism has come into the mainstream consciousness because of new age popularity in recent years. As with all things, minimalism has been severely misunderstood, misrepresented and misplaced to fit the narrative that is in the public bloodstream.

There are two ways in general to approach minimalism:

1. One is from their perspective and framework of stringent rules and guidelines. This can be rather restrictive, and frankly, it can become a pain. It usually results in the new practitioner to abandon the claustrophobic state of affairs and go back to the vagrancies of opulent spending – sometimes worse than what it was before the exercise in minimalistic living.

2. The second form of minimalism comes from the path of understanding. This takes a long time to institute, a significant amount of thought to understand, and requires a true appreciation of the eventual effects of the state. You see minimalism is not the new-age version of induced poverty or forced frugality, it is the understanding that happiness comes from within, and that

materialism and acquisition blunts and shields the soul to the point that we are no longer able to experience happiness.

Each of us is made of three conceptual parts. At any stage in our life, we are in different states in these three parts:

I.    We have the physical part of us. The part of us that we see as the body and physical appearance. Look at it this way: It's what you see when you look in the mirror.

II.    The second part of us is the mind – which more realistically is the center of the ego at this point. It tells us what it wants to see, how it wants us to look, whether we need to drive a Ferrari or have aesthetic alterations made to our physical body. This is commonly referred to as the ego. You can look at it as the entity that sees the vision of the body in the mirror.

III.    The third part is best described as the soul. It is the nexus between the universe and the mind/body pair. It thrives when the mind and body are in balance.

When you do not feed the body with nutrition, hydration, and air, it dies; if you don't feed the mind with intellectual sustenance, it erodes, then dies; finally, the soul – it too can die when we deprive it of peace and happiness. Understanding this truism will help you fully understand the effects, benefits, and nature of minimalism.

This is the path that we will traverse in this book – the path to budgets that foster minimalism, while assuring that the soul is happy and thriving. There are three areas that correspond to the three parts of our total self. Silence, peace and happiness relate to the soul. Living, fear, safety, food, and drink are areas that relate to the body. Appearance, power, control, egotistical issues, and worry, are all issues that cloud the mind.

# Consumption vs Greed

A good place to start to lay the foundation in understanding the nature of the body's most dangerous state is the need for consumption and the preoccupation of greed. The body is the absorption of the environment that surrounds it.

We consume the air from around us in the city, which we are internalizing as smog, in the country we internalize freshness – you can certainly tell the difference, right? We even internalize the water that we drink as part of our environment. When I stay home, the water I drink comes straight out of the tap and it is fine as I am used to it. When I traveled to India, the first time I drank out of the tap made me ill, but, to the locals, drinking out of the tap is fine.

Our body is in a state of balance at all times, and that balance changes depending on the surrounding that we subject our self to. The bacteria in our gut are in balance, and even the ones on our skin are in balance. Do you know that if you use too much antibacterial soap, researchers have found that it is counterproductive? That's because it changes the balance of bacteria colonies that live on our skin, and that is unhealthy. The same goes for the bacteria in our gut.

Consumption of nutrients is something the body naturally craves. When the body is in need of food, it alerts the conscious mind and the mind interprets that as being hungry and goes in search of food. Once you consume that food, you are rewarded with a sense of well-being, which we confuse as happiness. It is similar to, but not the same. It is more appropriate to refer to it as satiation than it is to refer to it as happiness.

That reward turns eating into a habit. That habit leads to gluttony and when we don't feed this habit, it makes us miserable. At that point, what was supposed to be a physical aspect of consumption turns into a mental state of consumption. The best way to adjust that is typically to fast. Fasting resets the body and clears the mind. It also allows you to take control of your habits. Now, this isn't a book about fasting and it wouldn't be fair to dive too deeply into it, but it is worth looking at because most people misunderstand fasting to mean the act that only has dietary consequences. It has more than that – it has significant mindset altering consequences.

Whenever I find that I am losing the plot in the play of life, I fast for a couple of days, and I find that my mind reverts to its balance. It is refreshing. It helps in my work and it keeps me positive.

The point we want to make about fasting here is not that you should or shouldn't, and that's up to you, but it is more about how you get to your mind of things. I will give you an example. Look at your pattern of eating. Most of us get hungry at around noon, and then again around 7 or 8. Would you think this is a body thing or a mental thing? Well, if you said "mind", you're right. Our hunger clock is something in the mind. It makes us 'feel' hungry based on a certain time of day because it is a habit that we are used to. If we miss the meal, we feel weak and lethargic but, more importantly, we feel a sense of peril. When you fast, for a day, or two to three days even, it first makes you realize that there is no doom or disaster when you don't eat for a day. You gain strength from knowing that you are not so fragile as to depend on something every few hours. You gain control over yourself from the knowledge that you do not need to constantly consume to be able to survive. When you do that, and at first it is hard, your mind eventually learns and then you become free from the nagging desire to fill your gut. The more you scrape off (in terms of unnecessary habits), the more you find yourself being happy for reasons that are real, and not happy from the rush of endorphin rewards initiated by the execution of a habit.

Think about that for a minute. Once again, fasting shows you how to extract more from life by not depending on superficial happiness created when you over-eat. This is the same thing that happens with minimalism. If you learn to wean yourself off material needs, you start to see the beauty of life in the way that gives you true happiness, and that is the real power of minimalism.

Unfortunately, the term minimalism has become the antithesis to success, while materialism and hoarding have become the personification of success and achievement. Hoarding and materialism form the core of greed. When you get underway on your path with greed as your guide, no matter what your achievement, it will never feel like it is enough and you will keep finding ever-deeper sadness when the endorphins fade. You will see more of this as we go through the book. When you start to understand this, then you will also start to understand the value of the golden ratio.

## Minimalism vs Frugalism

One way to understand minimalism is to look at it in comparison to other frequently confused concepts like frugalism. In frugalism, the person cuts and slashes costs and expenses down to the bone and then sometimes even more, but they do not know why they are doing this, and the reasons they conjure or rationalize it are not as fulfilling in the long term.

My mother was this kind of person. No matter how much we had, she would cut costs to the point of calculating when it was cheaper to drive somewhere or take the bus. It was infuriating at times when I couldn't get a penny out of her.

Frugalism is about tightening the belt to the point that you actually feel the pain of sacrifice. She would give more to the church in a month than she would spend on entertainment, travel and extras. We will talk about the power of giving later but, for now, let's stick to frugalism.

Frugalism is about being frugal – am sure you got that. What does that actually mean? There are two ways you can save. The first is to set a budget and follow that. The second is to consume without any budget, and then run out of funds by the next paycheck. We are all guilty of that at one point or another in our life. Being frugal is more conservative than just having a budget. It is to willfully and voluntarily spend less than the minimum amount the average person would normally spend.

I am a minimalist, but I am not frugal. I do not force myself to cut down because I want to save every penny. I reduce my consumption because I know that that is good for me. We will look at more of this in the book.

# Discipline

Discipline is something that we will see a lot in this book. It is an important aspect of all things that we do or need to accomplish. I look at discipline as something internally that compels me to do what I must, even in the face of resistance.

Before something becomes a habit, it needs to be willed. It needs to be forced because we do not know better and we need to teach ourselves what is good for us even if we do not know what that may be.

We tend to view discipline as something that is difficult to do and hard to invoke. That is primarily so because we seem to have taken it upon ourselves to think of discipline as something that needs enforcing, rather than something that requires refrain.

I have found that discipline is easier to enforce if you create a path rather than use brute force to bend. Let me put it to you this way: As the population of Rome grew, water and sanitation was a major concern as the rivers were not able to sufficiently feed the city. Instead of carrying water along long distances, they built aqueducts that tapped the water long distances away and, when gently placed on an inline, it would use gravity to bring fresh water into the city from the mountains far away. The amount of energy it would take to get slaves to do it would have been large, but building these aqueducts would gently allow water to reach the city. In essence, instead of putting in so much effort (by the slaves), they built a path for the water to flow and go their way.

In the same way, discipline is not about forcing yourself to do things, but rather it is about building a path that gets it done. It's all about the process. Everything in this world is a process – even your metabolism. Nothing ever goes from beginning to conclusion in one gigantic leap. They are done in millions of little steps, so discipline is not about forcing the occurrence of something, it is the wisdom to create a path so that thing you desire to see to fruition happens effortlessly – that is true discipline.

Here are many ways to create paths to the desired outcome, you need to think and reflect on the one that works best for you, and then create a path to it. That is all that it takes. In fact, if you visualize your outcome well, then the path that you need to create is conjured subconsciously and you end up following it without effort.

Minimalism is such an issue. It is the path that you take to allow happiness and peace to manifest in your life without having to put in the effort and the energy. If you just create the path, then the happiness and peace you deserve flow directly into your life, just like the water traversing the aqueducts of ancient Rome.

# Chapter 1: The Golden Ratio

The minimalist budget is not an arbitrary state of affairs. It is a well-defined, time-tested, and an effective practice that has positive consequences on every area of your life. It is based on the one thing that you cannot change in the short term – the amount of income that you generate.

If you earn $100 (an arbitrary number to illustrate the matter), then that is the limit of your budget. There are no two ways about it, unless you go out and do something or change your fortunes by making more, what you have is all you have; therefore, that's what you should live within. Stealing, cheating and borrowing are not allowed.

What you need to do with that $100 is to apportion it into three categories. The key is the ratio of the three categories and I will reveal that to you a couple of lines down in this chapter. A ratio is a simple thing to understand. You start off with the total of something and then you apportion them out to however many constituents there are. For instance, there are three parts in water – two hydrogen atoms and one oxygen atom (thus the H two O); the ratio of hydrogen to water is 2:1 (read two to one). There are a total of three parts (2 Hydrogen and 1 Oxygen) and the cumulative of each constituent cannot go above that total number.

In the same way, the golden ratio is the ratio of the constituents of your allocation. All the things that you apportion money to add up to one total number (like the three constituents in water) except, in this case, that number also represents your total net income.

We don't even need to look at taxes here because that's a given. You must pay your taxes right off the bat so there is no need to include that, and then subtracting that out again later so let's just start from a post-tax position. The ratio that works well at putting you on a path to happiness is a minimalism budget which is called the golden ratio.

The golden ratio is 60:30:10. That means 60% of your after-tax income goes to item A, 30% goes to item B, and 10% goes to item C. Items A, B and C are not individual lime items, but rather groups and categories of things that we all have in common.

The thing about items A, B, and C are that they change in time depending on the objective that you are trying to accomplish. The thing to note is that the ratio doesn't change, instead, the items do.

When you have debts (credit card balances, mortgages, car loans and personal loans, etc.) and you are just starting out on this golden ratio, item A is your debtor's list. That means you make 60% of your income go towards paying down your debtors.

You do this because a minimalist's budget is one where you spend what you can afford, and you never borrow to accomplish a purpose because your objective is to hold zero debt as quickly as possible. You will see the reason for this in the next chapter on debt but, for now, the idea is to build an understanding of the golden ratio. When you use the 60% of your income, it will accelerate your debt-reduction exercise and make you free.

It always astonishes me how much we value freedom, but to not see the shackles that debt places on us. It feels as though the extra temporary purchasing power that we are granted with debt is worth giving up our long-term freedom, but that statement only makes sense if your debt is from buying stuff. If your debt happens to be for medical bills, then it is, of course, a different story altogether. In any case, you need to pay it down as rapidly as possible. The 60% allocation will help you do that.

Then comes the 30% item B. That will go towards your living expenses. This, by the way, is a must. In many cases, this is going to be very hard, and I understand that. I have been there before but, let me tell you, holding on to debt is actually more dangerous and potentially more painful down the road. Living expenses must never exceed 30% of your income.

What does living expenses include? It includes everything that you need to survive. It includes food, shelter, transportation, communication, utilities and it even includes a little for going out on the town or having a drink with friends. If you make the minimum wage, let's say ten bucks an hour and work 40 hour weeks, that picture is going to look like this: $10 x 2,080 hours per year means that your income is $20,800 annually making your tax bill approximately $2,700. In monthly terms, you will be making about $1,500 per month.

That's your total income and so you apportion that out in the golden ratio 60:30:10 which is $900 to debt reduction, and $450 to living expenses.

Finally, you have item C which is to give away to charity. Giving away money when you need it the most is one of the most uplifting things that you will ever come across. Find a cause that is close to your heart and give it to that cause.

If you have elderly parents, you can give it to them too if you think it will raise the quality of their life but, in essence, the giving is to change your mindset from one of indifference to one of empowerment. When you give to others it is an empowering experience.

For the time that you have debt, this is the golden ratio that applies to you. You use this time to pay down all your debt and do not take on any more debt. We will visit the reasons behind this in the next chapter.

## Phase 1 – 60 is Debt Repayment

When you focus on repaying debt, three things happen:

1. You pay down debt rapidly, meaning the interest cost is lower. It also means that you can get out from under the burden of debt faster. This is not to say that you can take on debt up to the repayment of $900 (in this example).

2. You learn that surviving on a small amount every month is not only doable, but it also empowers you and makes you realize that you are capable of things you never thought possible.

3. Finally, it keeps you hungry. The best way to achieve supernatural feats in this world is by staying hungry. When you stay hungry, you tend to remain agile and light and your brain gets sharp. You tend to see things clearly and move from one step to the next at a pace that is faster and more certain.

When you only have $450 dollars to live on, you will get creative. When I did it, I did not do it because I wanted to be frugal, I did it because I had no other choice. I worked out the entire plan and I paid down my student loans and my credit card bill (yeah, the mistake I made in college). I spend $250 on rent – a room in an attic and cycled to work.

## Phase 2 – 60 is Savings

Once you get out of debt, and I have to tell you, that when I made that last payment on my student loans (I paid off the credit card balance first because of a higher interest rate), the exhilaration was more than I can explain. When you get out of debt you feel true freedom. You own no-one and there is nothing that you can't do because you overcame the greatest challenge a person can face but, now that you have all this extra cash, you will realize two things:

1. You have got used to living on a shoestring budget.

2. That entre chunk of 60% has nothing attached to it.

When you put those two together, what you find is that the best way forward is to save all that extra cash. In phase 2, 60% now goes towards savings, and the other two items continue growing towards living expenses and charity.

## Debt Service vs Repayment

While we are at, it is important that we revisit the issue of debt repayment and debt in general. Debt, in general, is not a good thing - even in the slightest. It has become the norm to spend based on debt. Credit cards are all over the place and there are even some places online that do not accept debit cards as payment and insist that one only uses a credit card. I typically do not use credit cards for any reason. I don't even have a credit card. Credit has become a bit of a status symbol and that is ironic. My mother-in-law was boasting to us when she visited the other day that her first daughter (my wife's older sister) just received a platinum supplementary card from the husband with a $250,000 credit line. She was telling us that the card was so 'powerful' it could pay for our entire house. My wife and I couldn't help but smile at each other. After grad school, my starting package (after tax) was $125,000 and I put away 60% of that every month. When my wife and I married, I had been working at this job for four years. The year after we were married, I bought our current home for cash. The following year (the great recession of 2008), our home value dipped but it did not affect us. Today, that same home is worth almost four times what I paid for it in cash.

The point is that savings have a compounding effect that you can't imagine until you are actually doing it. When you put off a purchase and save the money to make it at a later date, then you are not incurring the cost of interest in acquiring it right at this moment. That is the essence of minimalism and one of its true tests. You only buy what you really need and if you can afford it.

In my entire life, I've only purchased three phones. My first was a Motorola flip phone, my second was a Blackberry, and recently I bought a third Blackberry (and I bought it used for $29). I am not asking you to buy a Blackberry, I am just merely saying that my nature of minimalism dictates to me through this voice in my head, that I do not need to get something I don't need. I do not need a phone with an OLED screen, I do not need a phone that can convert my face into an emoji, and I don't need a phone that can scan my face. I need a phone to call my family, friends and, on occasion, the pizza guy.

When you take on debt to buy all these gadgets, two things are going on in the background:

1. The first is that you are over-estimating your worth and thereby satisfying your rewards before they are valid.

2. The second is that you are constantly in the hole of debt and never get a time in your life when you are out of it. That's a mentally debilitating feeling to have.

If you ever think about it, when the time comes to pay down your loans and debts, it takes a long time to do it because you have to now figure in the cost of interest. It takes you a shorter amount of time to purchase something with cash that you save, than it takes for you to pay off the debt of a borrowing you made to purchase an item on credit.

That brings us to the ultimate reason you should not take on debt. Putting aside all the reasons that make financial sense, the real reason you should not take on debt is that it alters the mind in a way that makes you forget that everything is a process. It makes you want things now. It feeds into instant gratification and it obfuscates the reality of life that consequence follows the action, and not the other way around.

# Frame of Mind

For your mind to be in the right frame, you need to be able to keep it clear that you have to work for a return and not take the return before the work. This is an important aspect of the mind. Once you start to show it that you can take the reward first without working for it, the mind subconsciously starts to behave in a way that is regressive in the long run. But, if you were to teach it, and affirm the fact that you have to work for the rewards and necessities that you desire, then you will place yourself in the mindset that always places a certain work ethic that will pay off in the short and long run. We will look at this in greater detail in the chapter on the minimalist mindset.

The golden ratio does two things for you in light of all we have discussed up to this point:

1. It forces you to adhere to the principles of deferred gratification. When you are in phase 1, you are forced to delay all comfort and enjoyment while you do what is responsible.

2. It allows you to advance your life by only one way – working for it.

Every single time that I have had the urge to buy something, I go through the process of reflection. I always ask myself why I want to buy it, and what my assumptions are about how my life would be after I acquire it. I find that when I do this, nothing seems to be urgent. As much as advertisers want to convey the message of urgency, the truth of the matter is that it is not something that is as urgent as it is made out to be.

When this is your frame of mind, you will find that you can stick to your budgets flawlessly and you are happier in the knowledge that your worth is not derived from the ownership of products, but by the contribution you make to the world around you.

There is a principle of life that comes into play and this forms the natural frame of mind that we are all a part of. This principle is that we all have a purpose and the rewards we draw from the fulfillment of that purpose is what sustains our existence. It is a natural balance in the universe.

This then feeds into the next level of how things work. You start small and you work your way up to the next level, then the next, and the next and, while you think you are working hard in inconsequential ways, what is actually happening is that you are building a habit of contribution and you are building an experience which, in turn, molds and shapes your mind.

No-one can become a CEO on the first day of kindergarten. You need to start with learning ABC and 123, and then you need to go on to build your vocabulary and the relationship between the numbers and then you go on to building your ability to communicate and so on. The path is a process just like the water coming down those Roman aqueducts. A minimalist's budget is the same way, it creates a path in your mind. It does these for you:

1. Sets your mindset to contribute first and reap the rewards later.

2. It allows you to build a path to success and greatness.

3. It defers gratification and teaches you to embrace contribution more than its reward.

4. It teaches you to contribute more if you want to make more.

The idea of contribution is one that baffles many of us who do not have an intimate relationship with minimalism and minimalist's budgets. Contribution is not the same as charity. Contribution is everything that we do and who we are. If I worked at a food joint, then my contribution is that I am part of the process that brings food to those who are in search of it. If I am a pilot, then I am part of the transportation infrastructure to get people from one place to another so that they can complete their contribution or enjoy their rewards. If I steal or borrow, I am not contributing in any way, in fact, I am short-circuiting the system and causing harm to everyone else.

If you steal, your actions harm someone else. Can you see that? Sure, that one is easy to see, but what about borrowing or taking on a mortgage to buy a house. That can't be bad in any way to someone else, can it? Yes, it can. Most of the houses that are sold are not based on cost plus, but based on demand. The more an item is demanded, the more it is priced, and if the consumer can meet that price, the price goes up further. The only way consumers can meet the exorbitant prices is if they borrow, or they defer the purchase and save the money to buy it for cash.

When a person borrows, they contribute towards the inflation of price. That makes it hard for someone who can't borrow to ever buy a house. This is when you have to force minimalism on yourself, save every penny and buy the house, but, because the developer is basing his price on demand, all those houses financed by debt is causing a demand that is not natural and so everyone has to pay for it by paying a demand-inflated price.

But we can't control everyone, and we can only seek to do what is right for ourselves. We will look at debt and the minimalist in the next chapter.

The bottom line of minimalism is not about best financial practices, although it can be. The bottom line of minimalism is about your frame of mind. If you can truly appreciate the path that your mindset creates then you will see that minimalism is not a hardship, it is a blessing.

# Chapter 2: Zero Debt

We talked briefly about zero debt in the last chapter, but we need to uncover more than what we have touched upon in order to see it for what it is. It may sound like a fancy new-age way of doing things, but zero debt is really about aligning the forces in your mind that is the result of nature.

In the Galapagos Islands there is a turtle that is able to stick its head out and raise it above its shell to reach branches, and on the island across there are turtles that can't lift their heads beyond just sticking it out of its shell. The two variant species developed over time and do you know why? Because, on one island, the shrubs were short enough for the turtles to get to and, on the other, the shrubs were a little taller. The turtles on the second island evolved to be able to reach further.

What does this have to do with zero debt? Zero debt forces you to work smarter and harder to achieve the things that you need to survive and, while you are in the midst of doing that, you find that there are three things that you need to learn – no matter how hard:

1. You need to adapt

2. You need to move

3. Or you die.


That is the essence of evolution. In the same way, if you don't borrow, then you need to either adapt to your situation in life, you need to move out of that situation in life, or you will die standing. Borrowing only delays the inevitable.

Let me give you an example. If you think that you can live on the minimum wage for the rest of your life, you are wrong. You can if you have to, but it becomes fairly miserable. Here is why:

When you are young and you are single, the minimum-wage is an improvement compared to the times that you were taking pocket money or an allowance from your parents. The minimum wage job you have gives you the initial freedom and the ability to do things independently, but you can't get married on the minimum wage. Don't believe me, then ask the millions of people who live a tough life and they will tell you that it is impossible to live on the minimum wage without borrowing money. That's where the vicious cycle begins.

Instead, if you start your life, or you train your children for their future where no debt is allowed, what you find is that you start saving for everything. My kids all have savings accounts for various purposes. They have a main account for buying a house and they have accounts for college and vehicles. Every penny they make from mowing the lawn, to gifts from gramps, gets placed in these accounts according to a certain ratio. Even their pocket money gets put away.

We have a deal with the kids that if they keep all their money, they can take food from home instead. What happens is that they are given an allowance to buy food at school. They started off saving a large chunk of that and they would keep just enough to get food and drinks. This automatically knocked out junk food from the list, but, instead, over time, they started taking food from home because it wasn't enough to place money in savings and buy food outside. We came to an understanding that they could save as much as they wanted and take food from home, but they couldn't take food from home and spend their money on junk outside. It turns out they liked the idea so much that all of their allowances now goes into the bank and they hitch a ride with me or her mother to school, and they are no longer shy of brown-bagging food from home.

It's never too early to get started on good habits. Back to zero debt.

The kids practice something that I am a huge proponent of – focused saving. In focused saving, focused saving forces you to look down the road, expand your vision and plan ahead for something in the future without obsessing about it. Instead of worrying about what your credit score is, you should worry about what your future plan is. When I got my current job, the HR department contacted me and said that there was something wrong with my application. They were planning on shortlisting me but the discrepancy had thrown it off track. Apparently, they had done a background on me and one of the things was a credit check. The credit check came back non-existent. That's because my last credit card was more than fifteen years ago – that had fallen off. I had no rent issues because I owned my house, which I bought for cash, and my car was also a cash purchase. I make it a habit to not support debt so I have no friends to whom I stand as a co-signer. Because of all of this, my credit report came back zero. This is apparently a problem. I had to make an effort to explain to the HR Director that my record was literally spotless because I practice minimalism and that really means zero debt.

When I practice zero debt, my frame of mind is one that directs me to purchase what I can afford when I shop. I don't get sold by the hype, I shop for what I need – even if that means not buying what is on offer. There is a strict discipline about shopping in our household. We don't go to the mall on the weekends, as we go to the club instead. Yeah, I know, it sounds odd to say that I am a minimalist but have a golf club membership. That membership came well within our savings.

## Focused Spending

We touched on focused spending earlier and now is a good time to look at it deeper in the context of zero debt. Focused spending is about expenses that you willfully and consciously make. It requires a tremendous amount of discipline to execute, but it is worth it in the long run. We make detailed grocery lists when we go shopping and we stick to it regardless of the different offers they have. We purchase in bulk what we think is worth it, but we purchase just what is needed at other times. There is a clear and deliberate path to our consumption.

The biggest tip that I can give you about being a minimalist is to change your frame of mind so that what you are doing doesn't need the effort that goes into doing things that you force yourself into doing.

My father once told me a story of the beggar and the fisherman. The fisherman was returning to shore on his little boat with the catch of the day. On the beach was a beggar who asked him if the fisherman could spare him a fish. He was hungry and had no means to get food. The fisherman gave him a fish and went on his way. The next day, as he returned to shore, he saw the same man. After a short conversation, he gave him another fish. On the third day, the man was waiting for the fisherman on his return. He gave him the fish just like he had done on two earlier occasions, except this time, he told him that that would be the last time he gave him fish, but he would instead teach the man how to fish if he would come the next day at dawn. The man showed up, they went out together on the boat and the man learned how to fish. He never went hungry after that day.

The story is simplistic and obviously designed to narrate the saying "Give a man a fish, he eats for a day, teach a man to fish, he eats for a lifetime". The point is that I don't just want to give you the steps on how to make a minimalist budget, I want to give you the steps to construct the framework that you need to build your own so that the principles that you lay out will serve you well, and the practices that you develop will see you through hard times.

How does this relate to zero debt? Zero debt is the art of learning how to fish. If you can learn to live life without having to borrow money, you will find that you reach stratospheric heights of accomplishment – that is the quintessential core of minimalism. Minimalism is not about being stagnant and poor. It is about being upwardly mobile. The lighter you are, the further you climb. Spending is a hurdle. It creates unwanted burdens and erects tall barriers. Spending is a distraction. That is why you need to focus your spending and make it just about the essentials. If you allow spending to overwhelm you, it will distract you from your path.

The other issue with spending is that once you get used to it, whenever you feel down, you need to spend your way out of it and that becomes an addiction. An addiction will distract you from your work and your happiness. The best way to counter it is minimalism because, if you practice minimalism, then you will never be at risk of turning to retail therapy for your solace. Focused spending is about spending on things that are necessary. You buy a car to drive it from A to B, not to show it off. You buy clothes to protect your decency, and not to inflate your ego. You buy clean and healthy food, regardless of the brand affiliation. Focused spending is about the exchange of goods and services, not the inflation of ego.

If you spend on any other reason, then you will be tempted to borrow to spend and that is not a path that will lead to good things.

# Mindful Wanting

Mindful wanting sits on the other side of the coin from focused spending. If you are mindful of your desires, then you can focus your spending in a way that is effective. Being mindful of your desires and wants is a good place to start. If you think that accomplishment is about dreaming of your rewards or how you are going to spend it, then you are in for a world of hurt. People like Gates and Bezos did not set up their business to be the richest person on earth, they set it up to do big things, and they worked hard at it. Steve Jobs didn't sell his VW bus because he had dreams of grandeur of how wealthy his company or he would become but, rather, he built a company that added value, and contributed trillions in value to people around the world. I write on a Mac at home, and all the computers at work are either Macs or iPads. The amount of value generated by something that streamed directly from Steve Jobs' hands is incalculable, and that is why his legacy is on track to becoming the world's first trillion dollar company. If he had even, for a second, focused on the monetary aspect of it, it wouldn't have come this far.

Let's be clear. I am not saying that he is not thinking about money at all. Of course he his, and so are all of them, but they are not focusing on which Bentley or Rolls Royce they are going to purchase; they are fixated on the contribution they are making.

From that perspective you need to keep your wants and desire in check. Minimalism creates the guardrails along your path that help you do that. It helps you focus on what is important.

When you want something, be mindful of it. Make sure it is not something that you are convinced unnecessarily to acquire. Block yourself out from commercials and advertisements. Be aware of the appreciation by association. Don't fall for the tricks of slick advertisers to convince you that you need to buy something that you don't need and to pay for it by borrowing money that you don't have. Do you realize how silly that is? Don't fall for it. Be mindful of what is being planted in your head. Reflect on each notion and each desire. Ask yourself if it is something you really need.

I told you earlier that I bought a second-hand Blackberry recently, my third smartphone in all my life. The story started out a little differently though. I was sold on the iPhone X. I was sold on the look and on the performance. I was sold on the interconnectivity and the fact that I could access my work on the go. I came close to purchasing it, but then I stopped. This habit in me that I had been cultivating for almost 25 years kicked in and shook me up. I asked myself what of those features would I really use and really need. I found there was none. In fact, the iPhone X even had one disadvantage. I am not a soft keyboard kind of person. I was willing to overlook that and take on the iPhone because I could never key in a soft pad. When I finally reflected on what I wanted, it turned out that the Blackberry was the best option, and so I found a $29 one on eBay. Look at the difference - $999 to $29. I just saved $970 and I can still send messages, make calls and go online when I need to at home.

I am not a Blackberry evangelist. If anything, I am an Apple and a Steve Jobs' fan, but I bring this up to illustrate what a few minutes of thinking and reflecting can save you a lot. Mind you, this is not an instance of me forcing myself not to spend. It is about coming into the light and seeking the truth of the matter. When you contemplate all your purchases, you will come to realize that there is a lot that you can do without, and it's not just because you don't want to pay more for it, but it actually becomes more of a burden than it does actually help.

A friend of mine and I traveled to London for our internship back during grad school. I packed a garment bag and a weekender along with my laptop sling (which was pretty big back then). She went shopping for the trip and bought expensive luggage.

Both her expensive luggage and my old garment carrier served the same purpose, except hers caused her a lot more grief when they were lost in transit. She ended up spending more time worrying about her luggage than the things inside. It's another distraction that you don't need in your march to the top.

In that way, it is just like debt. You can't keep a straight face and honestly tell me that your debt burden is ok with you. How many times have you thought of jumping jobs or taking on a certain kind of risk, but you stop short when you think about the obligations you have in terms of debt. Debts can ensnare you into situations that you have no idea about and are around the corner or beyond the horizon. When you have no debt to think of, you are left hungry and focused.

The idea of staying hungry is the way you condition yourself to want more than you have. When you have nothing, it is very easy to strive for more but, when you have it all, it's hard to get off the lap of comfort and luxury to go out and do what is necessary. Whether you are a minimalist or not, staying hungry is a highly effective and powerful strategy. The opposite of it is the kind of person that flaunts what they don't have and uses borrowed resources to fool the world. There is no benefit in that for the real person but, to a person who lives in his ego, then that is all he needs. It eventually comes crashing down.

# Debt is Expensive

Whatever rate you are paying for your loan, mortgage or borrowing, let me tell you it's too much. Borrowing in companies is a different thing than borrowing as an individual. Debt for companies can be encouraged to a certain extent but, for the individual, the needs and desires are different and should be avoided at all costs. There are three costs to be paid for the debt. We have already looked at one up to this point, but let me reiterate and mention the other three. The three are:

1. A burden that is a distraction and the fact that debt purchases gives the person a sense of false well-being.

2. Debt costs more than saving. Let me give you an example. In 2013, the price of the Corvette 2 Door Coupe Grand Sport was $56,000. If I put 10% down and financed it for 5 years, my monthly payments would be about $900. Over five years that would add up to $54,000. Including the down payment of 10%, that would make my total cash outlay of $59,500. In 2018, the price of the current year model is $56,000 – which is not so much different than the car's price five years earlier. If I saved $900 every month at a rate of 1.2% per annum, I would make $1620 in interest and, in 5 years, I would have been able to save the amount I needed to make the purchase. I could walk in and buy the car for cash.

3. Debt is expensive because it ties you down. If you bought a car today and needed to sell it tomorrow, you would have to fork out money just so that you didn't owe anyone.

The problem with these issues is that society doesn't look at things in this way anymore. They look at instant gratification and getting into the car today rather than putting it off in five years. The good thing about putting it off for five years is that when the time comes, you would probably change your mind, and you know what you have instead – you have an extra $56,000 in the bank. That's not a bad thing at all.

Buying the Corvette is also not a minimalist's thing in the first place. As you get more comfortable in your own skin and you start to care less about what others think, you start to understand that it is your contribution that matters, and the fact that you borrowed money to get yourself distracted, does not make any kind of sense. If you stayed hungry as a minimalist and you put off the grandeur and traded it instead of humility and focus, what you will achieve is so much more than the trappings of luxury and the illusion of accomplishment that borrowed money gives you.

## Chapter 3: Minimalist Mindset

Let me condense it down for you. A minimalist's budget starts in his soul once you understand why you need to do it, and what it gets you. Once you do, then you will be able to put together a budget that follows the golden ratio perfectly and worthy of your state.

No series of lists or guidelines will help you if you don't get your mindset in order but, regardless, I shall still distill it down into a list that you can tick off, but do so only with the understanding of the mindset that needs to stand behind this action.

What you have up to this point is the understanding that a minimalist mindset gets you on the path to achievement and success. You also know that the golden ratio is two separate scenarios – in debt and without debt. You also know that minimalism allows you to be undistracted – a crucial component in aspiring for success.

Now, what you need is to get on your way to building a budget that is within the framework of the golden ratio and then you will be able to get on your way to experience the joys of life.

I just want to take on the point of personal privilege here. When I was doing this to pay down my sole credit card and student loan, there were a number of times that was really hard. No-one was holding a gun to my head and I was ahead of all my payments. I could spend a little and feel good.

All I had to do was stop and think and the notion would remind me that I didn't need to spend to feel good so I decided there must be other ways to do it, and I did. You need to remember in your heart that a minimalist mindset doesn't preclude you from playing golf – it precludes you from buying fancy equipment that you don't need. I still play with used clubs that I got from my neighborhood Play it Again Sports store. If I ruin a club, I just go back to the store and find a replacement. Being a minimalist reminds me to enjoy the game, not the gadgets. Being a minimalist demands that I focus on what is important and not on what is fancy or what is external.

# The Minimalist's Budget

It is incorrect to assume that there is only one kind of budget or there is a group of budgets that characterize the minimalist's mindset. Instead, look at a minimalist's mindset in a way that is holistic – that means you look at it as part of who you are, how you breathe, what you consume, the way you walk, and even the way you talk – it is almost a Stoic experience. In fact, minimalism is a branch of Stoicism – and Stoicism is the root of conduct for some of the most successful souls in the world today. They may not profess a union with some Stoic order (because there are none), but their conduct, mindset and values are Stoic in nature.

The minimalist's budget does two things (in addition to all the things we have already talked about):

1. It reduces waste by preventing impulse purchases.

2. It clears the mind from the predisposition of acquisition.

Minimalist budgets are strict because they start with a percentage that almost seems arbitrary. It includes large amounts that go towards saving, and it includes a small amount that goes toward charity, even during times that you feel that you could use a little charity yourself. But when you stick to a minimalist's budget, even in the face of disbelief, you start to see that the savings you build up, or the debt you break down, starts to build the confidence in you that life has nothing to do with possessions. It has, instead, all to do with contribution.

Let's start by talking about the giving that is built into the minimalist's budget. That giving feels like it tears away from your hard-earned money, but the universe has always been a place where I've found that the more you give, the more you get. This is not to say that you should choose to give only because it gives you a reward. No. Instead, choose to give because you take responsibility for the world around you and in your own way. Giving allows you to see the universe in a way that differs from takers. Takers are usually looking to see how they can scam the system or take what does not always belong to them. Giving prevents that kind of mindset.

On the other hand, when you build giving into the budget, you create a source that perpetuates hunger in you (not physical hunger). This is a healthy act that satisfies the soul on a very deep level and bestows peace and happiness.

Peace and happiness are two areas that are generated by minimalism and, in turn, create an understanding of the universe, the laws of attraction and the manifestation of abundance. In many of the texts that talk about these laws and phenomenon, the one thing that I never see accompany them is the discussion of minimalism. I believe that part of the reason behind this is that the typical market associates the satisfaction of success with the amount of reward and purchasing power that comes with it.

These are some of the qualitative aspects of the minimalist's budget. What are the quantitative aspects?

Quantitatively, minimalism is based on the mindful reverence for what you spend. Minimalism teaches you to mind your spending and, to do that, you have to give yourself a strict cut-off point of what you can spend and how you can spend it. If you reach the point of insufficiency, then what you need to do is think of a way to make more money, not think of how to change the budget. That golden ratio is absolute. You must not even think of changing it.

# Charity

To whom you direct your charity is not as important as you make up your mind to give it no matter what happens. When I started giving to charity as a matter of practice, it dawned on me that the only way that I could have a little more to spend on other things was to go out and make more money. It created a palpable hunger that was so deep that eventually, I found ways to improve myself and keep advancing my career. I advance my rate of contribution in terms of the work I did, and in terms of the funds I gave away. Spending hard-earned money on flashy things has a different effect. It does not allow you to value your contribution. It only cheapens your effort to the tune of the inconsequential things that you buy. Most of these things eventually are worthless and that has a bearing on your subconscious psyche. However, charity has a different effect. It makes you grow inside. It shows you your ability and your place in this universe and it gives you the impetus to get up and do more. Charity that is not forced has the best long-term effect within us, and it is something that you must do right away without calculating the potential return on investment. That is the true value of charitable giving – the benefit accrues to the giver more than to the recipient.

# Chapter 4: Tips on Minimalist Budgeting

The first few months of cutting back on consumption can be jarring to the system. We have lived most of our lives, from the first moments we are exposed to media, to the point we are here at this moment in time. Much of our consumption patterns aren't dictated by what we need, but rather hypnotically suggested by what we consume in terms of media content. The power of suggestion through advertising, the insurmountable power of association in commercial advertisement, the persuasive power of peer pressure, and the internal genetic code that is designed to spread conformity, all pull together to make us susceptible to consumption.

To live a minimalist lifestyle and to create, perfect and enforce a minimalist budget, the first thing we need to do is shield ourselves from these consumption-centric philosophies and the constant bombardment of suggestions to consume things we do not need. The best way they have to influence our consumption patterns is to tell us we won't be happy until we buy something, use it, and make a habit out of it.

There are two ways to shield our minds from these assaults:

1. The first is, of course, to have a strict rule of what you buy and when you buy it. This closes our minds to external attempts to convince us of a product or service.

2. The second rule is to evaluate each item and determine if it indeed does have some utility and if that utility is cost effective.

The first shields us with discipline, while the second shields us with logic. In as far as discipline goes, the best way to get it going is to start with lists. Make a list for everything, and stick to it. If it doesn't work well, alter the list and then try it again but, whatever you do, do not deviate from the list. Let's say you make a grocery list, and when you get to the store two things happen. The first is that you see something that you want but is not on the list because you forgot to put it on. The second thing that happens is that you see something that you don't want, or need now, but will in the future, and it's not on your list this week but will be on next week's list – and this item happens to be on sale.

In these two scenarios, the outcome is the same – you do not deviate from the list. You are trying to create a wall – a type of barrier that enforces your resolve and immunity to outside attempts at persuasion. For this reason, you create a list out of need and you stick to it. The best time to go shopping is on a full stomach and at home. When you have a full stomach and you are at home, you are going to base that grocery list on need rather than impulse or fancy.

In the same way that you prepare lists for groceries, rely on lists for other bills as well and plan ahead. Always look a year in advance for expenditure. Until today, I map out all my expenses, including birthday gifts for members of my family, holiday gifts, and even upcoming weddings that we've been invited to. Even our vacation is mapped out and budget taken into account. By doing all these things, I know what to cut back on at other times of the year and put the funds forward for that occasion. In the last 25 years, I have never gone over my 30% budget for living expenses and incidentals.

# The Envelope System

This is not exclusively a minimalist's strategy, but I have used this for ages and it works very well. You should divide all your budgets into envelopes. I have a savings envelope, a charity envelope and a large envelope for my expenses. Inside the expenses envelope, I have multiple smaller envelopes - each for a particular week of the month and for a particular task.

My expenses envelope will carry no more than 30% of my take-home income. Within that, it is divided into function and then again by week if necessary. For instance, the total grocery budget for the month will be divided into four, representing the money needed to get what is needed for that particular week. The utilities envelop will carry the allocation for the utility bills, and the other envelopes will also be marked accordingly. Those are then placed in a filing system based on when they are due. If I have to save for a club bill that is coming up in three months, then that money comes out of my expenses budget and goes into a reservoir envelope for the club bill.

In the same way, if I plan on buying a car, I create a car envelope and I take the money coming from my monthly expenses (just as though I would if I had to pay a car loan). Then I take the money out of the month's budget and put it in there. So, let's say I have two years to save up twelve thousand dollars, then I start taking five hundred every month out of the expenses budget and putting it in this envelope. At the end of two years, I now have twelve thousand dollars I can use to buy a car.

## Savings Begets Savings

Even though I talked about banks earlier and savings' interest rates, I don't use banks, but you can, and a lot of people do. I have a bank account that is used to collect paychecks and investment returns, but my cash is converted into two asset classes and stored at home. I am always liquid and never need to rely on a bank for my needs.

I have no need to spend large amounts of resources on home protection because it is a modest home and the car in the garage is a modest car that I purchased used. We dress simple, we have no outward appearance of wealth, and we remain content with a twelve-year-old car, and all of it is paid for. My car gets me from point A to B, just as a rich man's limousine. My home shelters me from the elements, and gives me my privacy, just like the King's castle. My kitchen is clean and stocked with the food I need and that is where I eat every day without the need to subject my gut to food prepared by a stranger using poor ingredients yet charging richly.

My sixty percent saving has not been touched. It has been converted to other assets and those assets have appreciated in value giving me a handsome return, but that is not of interest to me. I convert them to gold and property for two reasons:

1. The gold is a barrier that prevents me from spending the cash I save (because it's a bit of a hassle to convert back to cash compared to pounding keys at the ATM). Gold also seems to be appreciating in value above inflation so my purchasing power has never been eroded.

2. The property that I purchase with savings gives me an income that is then saved as well. It gives me a larger income to work with, and allows me to

increase my charity even though the percentage has stayed the same. Stealing it is also not so easily accomplished.

These two reasons for converting our savings out of cash has proven over time to keep me in check and maintained my minimalist lifestyle. I never go back and count how much I have accumulated in terms of savings. I find that to be unnecessary. What I do know is that between the savings that I have accumulated and the expenses that I limit myself to and the charity I give away, the greatest thing that it has benefited me is in the happiness and peace that a life not projected from consumption has given me.

# Chapter 5: Tips to Reduce Spending

The book is covered with tips in the form of mindset changes that you can make to control the way you spend, the way you save and the way you give. The biggest influence you can have on all three areas is made possible by altering and enhancing your mindset. Once you do that, you will be surprised to find that you will come up with so many ingenious ways to save on expenses and costs. Here are just a few that I have picked up along the way:

1. Don't borrow as the interest cost is savings that are huge.

2. Never buy on impulse, no matter how cheap the sale or offer is.

3. Always buy used (especially cars and electronics). My computer, phone and car are all previously owned. That way, I do not pay for the initial depreciation hit.

4. Don't throw away things you can't use. Sell them. I usually sell whatever I can't use. When my Blackberry stopped working and I was planning to buy the iPhone X (and eventually got another used Blackberry), I didn't just discard my old Blackberry, as I sold it for parts.

5. When your car has driven its last mile and is no longer cost-effective, either sell your car and recover its residual value, or donate the car and get a tax write-off.

6. Don't do all your shopping in bulk stores like Costco. Some things are worth it, others are not. Think before deciding.

7. Make lists for everything.

8. Plan ahead... way ahead.

9. Set aside a rainy day fund from within your expenses budget.

10. Think of the savings portion (the 60%) as something that you are never going to touch. You have to remember that the minimalist is trying to save his soul not buy something big at the end of ten years. Saving the 60% is about learning to live with just the right amount. The fact that you create a wealth in the background is secondary.

11. Buy what you can online, it is sometimes cheaper even when you include shipping.

## Reciting a Mantra

I have a mantra that has been with me for the last twenty-something years. It is something that I recite every morning. I have it committed so deep within me that I find myself reciting it whenever I am in need of a calming voice.

The mantra is not religious in any way. It is purely a secular matter that lines up your mind and your present to the day before you and the task at hand. It creates the strength you need to do what you must, and the discipline to think in a way that protects your values. A mantra is a powerful thing. Mine is based on Marcus Aurelius' Meditations, and it gives me the resolve I need every day and at any moment.

You need one of these mantras that you can recite even before your eyes greet the light of a new day. Something that starts from a piece of paper that you write in your most inspired state then moves to the annals of your memories, then wedges itself inextricably within the rock face of your value system.

# Meditating

The need to meditate is not exclusive to Stoics and minimalists or Zen monks. The need for reflection and meditation is one of the greatest aspects of keeping yourself in a state of stable calmness.

Minimalist budgets are really trying to accomplish two things. The first is that it is trying to protect you from your need to spend and extract pleasure and fleeting happiness from that spending habit. The second is that it is trying to keep your mindset calm so that you find that happiness is not made up of pleasures, but rather made up of something more profound.

Meditation finally reveals to the minimalist that there is no happiness and there never will be happiness in the act of buying, even when it is the act of buying something you need. Meditation shows you that true happiness comes from within and the way you see all things around you and how you see yourself. If you need an expensive Hermes handbag, then that is all you are worth but, if you can see happiness beyond any object, then you are worth more than you can imagine.

Minimalist budgets are designed to advance that truism. Minimalist budgets force you, at first, to see the value of your life beyond the mere marketing ploys of meaningless products. How could you possibly do anything great if you compare your value to a hunk of steel and aluminum?

Remember that minimalism is not a fad. It's not a race to see who can live with the least amount of goods and services, or how we can wear the badge of pride to say 'look at me, I am a minimalist and that makes me smarter or more blessed than you.' No, that is not what minimalism is about. Minimalism is about stoking the real fire within you. It is about removing the consumption of goods and services that dull the physical senses, or inflate the mind's ego to the point that it blots out the spirit's peace.

The greatest tip I can give you for your budget is to tell you that no matter what you think you need, you don't. Look at everything as a tool to serve its purpose. If you can't fathom that, try it this way – a car is to reliably take me from point A to point B. That's all I need it to do. If I have to pay even a penny more so that it can keep my kids entertained with cartoons in the back, then that is a penny too much.

# Conclusion

Minimalism is not a strain on your mind or soul. It is the liberator of it. Minimalist budgets are not budgets to restrict your fun; it is the path to extract happiness. Minimalist's budgets are not there to handicap you by curtailing your acquisition of stuff, it is the tool to highlight your self-sufficiency and your independence from things that are not needed to live a life that is happy and peaceful. As the great Gandhi once said, *"The world has more than enough for our needs, but nearly enough for our wants."*

Borrowing is anathema to the minimalist's budget. A minimalist is looking to live within his means. The very act of borrowing means that he is living beyond what he earns today. You have to live in the moment. You spend what you have and you acquire what you have worked for. That is the natural order that the soul in you is content with.

The natural order of things does not include the calculus of debt and the spending that which you do not rightfully earn or acquire. It is in our genes. We have to hunt for our food or pay someone to do it. To be able to pay for that doesn't mean we do nothing and then get someone to hunt in our stead. We, in turn, have to do something else and get paid. The value for work is transmitted through currency and that gives us the right to purchase what we need and what we deserve. You can't sit down and live off debt as it will come back to haunt you in unimaginable ways. Minimalism prevents that.

The extraction of 70% of all that we earn is not arbitrary in any way. It is the right balance of what we earn versus what we need to make in order to survive to live a simple existence. The less we learn to live with, the more efficient and effective our body becomes. When you start to live large, your mental frame shifts and you are no longer in the mindset that supports advancement. This is the essence of remaining hungry. When I first started my life as a minimalist, it took some time, but then I saw how effective I became and how driven I was, and the idea of being a minimalist appealed to me in a whole different way.

The key to a minimalist's budget is that you learn to sharpen and live by your own devices. You first remove debt so that you can see that you can do it on your own. You do not need the price of buying a fancy house as you can live in a room in an apartment building. As long as you keep yourself clean and healthy, it is all that matters.

Cutting out the noise that pushes you towards vanity and spending is as important as cutting out the spending because what you are trying to do is see minimalism for what it is, and not just spend your entire life feeling sorry for yourself that you have to be minimalist so that you can survive. You shouldn't be forced into living minimally, you should do it wholeheartedly and see how much you flourish.

Being a minimalist is the richest experience I have ever had and, more often than not, it is the resolve that kept the faith, but when the light was the dimmest, it was the budget that fed the flames until my own discipline took over and my own spirit fueled the flame.

www.ingramcontent.com/pod-product-compliance
Lightning Source LLC
Chambersburg PA
CBHW051334220526
45468CB00004B/1639